Thomas Edison
Practical Genius

Steven Jay Griffel

PEARSON

Boston, Massachusetts
Chandler, Arizona
Glenview, Illinois
Upper Saddle River, New Jersey

Photographs

Every effort has been made to secure permission and provide appropriate credit for photographic material. The publisher deeply regrets any omission and pledges to correct errors called to its attention in subsequent editions.

Unless otherwise acknowledged, all photographs are the property of Pearson Education, Inc.

Photo locators denoted as follows: Top (T), Center (C), Bottom (B), Left (L), Right (R), Background (Bkgd)

Opener: Prints & Photographs Division, LC-USZ62-98066/Library of Congress; 1 Prints & Photographs Division, LC-USZ62-98066/Library of Congress; 2 HABS OHIO, 22-MILA,1, Historic American Buildings Survey, Prints & Photographs Division/Library of Congress; 3 Prints & Photographs Division, LC-USZ62-55326/Library of Congress; 4 Prints & Photographs Division, LC-USZ62-110409/Library of Congress; 5 Courtesy of U.S. Dept. of the Interior, National Park Service, Thomas Edison National Historical Park/The National Park Service; 6 Thomas Edison National Historical Park, National Park Service/The National Park Service; 8 Detroit Publishing Company Photograph Collection, Prints & Photographs Division, LC-DIG-det-4a27975/Library of Congress; 9 Brady-Handy Collection, Prints & Photographs Division, LC-DIG-cwpbh-04044/Library of Congress; 10 PH Filing Series Photographs Collection, Prints & Photographs Division, LC-DIG-ppmsca-13462/Library of Congress; 11 Courtesy of U.S. Dept. of the Interior, National Park Service, Thomas Edison National Historical Park/The National Park Service; 12 Courtesy of U.S. Dept. of the Interior, National Park Service, Thomas Edison National Historical Park/The National Park Service; 13 Prints & Photographs Division, LC-USZ62-98068/Library of Congress; 14 Prints & Photographs Division, LC-USZ62-103830/Library of Congress; 15 Courtesy of U.S. Dept. of the Interior, National Park Service, Thomas Edison National Historical Park/The National Park Service.

ISBN-13: 978-0-328-67712-2
ISBN-10: 0-328-67712-4

6 7 8 9 V0SI 18 17 16 15

The Young Inventor

What does it take to be a great inventor? Thomas Edison believed that good ideas are important, but the real key to invention is hard work. Edison was one inventor who definitely worked hard. When he died in 1931, he had built an invention business that produced more than a thousand inventions. In so doing, Edison changed the way many people live.

For a great inventor, Thomas Edison had quite ordinary beginnings. He was born on February 11, 1847, in Milan, Ohio. His father was a builder, and his mother was a schoolteacher.

As a boy, Edison was curious and asked a lot of questions. In fact, he asked so many questions that his teachers thought he was a slow learner. Edison grew to dislike school, so his mother began to teach him at home. With her encouragement, Edison read a lot about history and science. But the book that really inspired the young inventor was a collection of experiments his mother gave him. Edison set up a laboratory in the basement of his home and conducted every experiment in the book. At times, the resulting explosions shook his house.

Edison grew up in this house in Milan, Ohio.

Edison Rides the Rails

As a boy, Thomas Edison was always asking questions.

Like many other children at the time, Edison began working at a young age. He sold newspapers on a train when he was just 12. Young Edison was looking for adventure, but he had a plan to make money. He also convinced his boss to let him bring fruit and sandwiches on board the train. Then he hired two boys to sell the food. With the **profits** he made, Edison bought chemicals for a laboratory that he had set up in the train's baggage car.

Unfortunately, one day, the train hit a bump. Edison's experiments went flying, resulting in a fire in the baggage car. The conductor was angry and kicked Edison, his newspapers, and his laboratory out at the next station. But somehow, Edison managed to keep his job.

Edison's Hearing Loss

Thomas Edison suffered from partial deafness that he said was caused by an accident. According to Edison, one day he was trying to climb into a train with an armful of newspapers when a conductor saw him and lifted him by both ears. Edison felt something snap in his head, and soon after, his deafness began. The incident probably left him with sore ears, but doctors doubt that it caused his hearing loss. Instead, Edison most likely lost his hearing because of a childhood illness.

A Coded Message

Edison continued to work on the trains, until one event changed everything. While at work one day, he rescued the manager's young son from the path of a slow-moving train. The boy's father was so grateful that he offered to teach Edison about **telegraphy**—how to send and receive Morse code messages. Morse code is a system of short and long electronic signals, called dots and dashes, used to send messages over telegraph wires.

Operating a telegraph was a difficult skill to learn. A telegraph operator needed to be able to think and respond quickly in order to turn the dots and dashes of Morse code into words and sentences. But Edison learned the skill, and at the age of 16, he became a telegraph operator.

In addition to operating the telegraph, Edison was also responsible for keeping the equipment working. He spent long hours taking apart telegraph equipment and putting it back together, just to understand how it worked. In this way, he learned a lot about electricity as well. Before long, he even began thinking about ways to improve the telegraph.

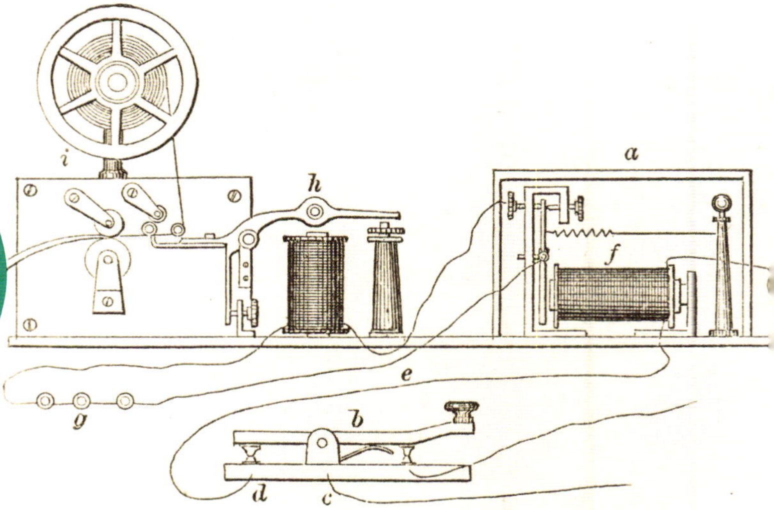

Telegraph equipment sent electronic messages over wires.

An Invention Business

Edison's vote recorder was never used.

After a few years as a telegrapher, Edison began working on his first invention. In 1869, he received a **patent** for an electronic vote recorder for Congress. A patent is a legal document that prevents others from copying an invention and making money from it. The machine worked well but Congress did not want it. Edison's vote recorder was never used, but the experience taught him an important lesson: make sure an invention is wanted or needed before you begin.

Out of money and out of work, Edison moved to New York. He was 21, and he was about to get another big break. He was working in an office when the telegraph equipment broke down. The office workers relied on the telegraph to send out fast-changing prices to other businesses. Without the equipment, office workers were in a panic.

Edison's knowledge of telegraph equipment proved useful. He was able to repair the machine within two hours. He became a hero to the people he worked with. Later, he made improvements to the telegraph equipment and was paid $40,000 by the telegraph company for his work.

Edison used the money to set up a laboratory and factory in Newark, New Jersey. He hired three assistants, and before long they began producing many money-making inventions.

Family Life

Thomas A. Edison with his children Charles and Madeleine

Around this time, in 1871, Edison married Mary Stilwell, a young woman who was working in his Newark laboratory. They had three children, named Marion, Thomas, Jr., and William.

Mary Edison died in August, 1884. Nearly two years later, Edison married Mina Miller. The couple also had three children, named Madeleine, Charles, and Theodore. Madeleine later ran for Congress, though she was not elected. Charles became governor of New Jersey and took charge of his father's laboratories. Theodore became an inventor.

Edison did not spend a lot of time with his family. When he was home he was usually busy with his experiments and often went about in old work clothes. He rarely ate meals with his wife and children and instead stayed in the laboratory. In fact, Edison was so focused on his work that sometimes he worked right through the night. "I owe my success," he once said, "to the fact that I never had a clock in my workroom."

Famous Sayings of Thomas Edison:

Edison was known for his wise and sometimes funny sayings. You may have already heard some of these.

"Just because something doesn't do what you planned it to do doesn't mean it's useless."

"Many of life's failures are people who did not realize how close they were to success when they gave up."

"Opportunity is missed by most people because it is dressed in overalls and looks like work."

"To invent, you need a good imagination and a pile of junk."

The Invention Factory

In 1876, Edison began his biggest project to date, a new laboratory at Menlo Park, New Jersey. Here, Edison put together a team of many scientists and engineers who came from all around the world. They had the skills to turn Edison's ideas into real devices.

Work at Menlo Park was difficult, and Edison expected his employees to work long hours. But Edison worked right alongside his employees, often well into the night. On those late nights, the inventor often encouraged his employees to take a break around midnight and join him around the piano to sing songs.

Menlo Park was the first of its kind, a laboratory devoted entirely to the invention of useful products. Here scientists worked on dozens of inventions at a time. Some people say that Menlo Park was Edison's greatest invention. There, he began to change the world.

The Telephone

Thomas Edison was well-known for his knowledge of telegraphy, so when a company wanted to develop a "speaking telegraph," they asked Edison to help. Edison worked hard on the project and came close to inventing the first telephone. However, Alexander Graham Bell received a patent for the first telephone in 1876.

Rarely discouraged, Edison worked to improve Bell's invention. The sound sent out by Bell's telephone was weak and full of static. Edison solved the problem. He developed a button-size **transmitter** that sent clear, strong sound through the wires, even over long distances. That transmitter is still used in some telephones today.

Demonstrating Bell's first telephone

"Hello!"

According to one story, Edison was impatient to test his new transmitter. Instead of speaking into the phone with what was the usual greeting of "Are you there?" he picked up the telephone and shouted, "Hello!" Before long, this became the usual way to start a telephone conversation.

The Talking Machine

This early phonograph recorded sound on a tinfoil tube.

Of all of Edison's inventions, his favorite was the phonograph. He called it a "talking machine." Basically, it was a big, hand-rotated tube wrapped in tinfoil. When Edison spoke into a mouthpiece, the vibration of his voice caused the sharp point of a needle to cut a trace in the tinfoil. Another needle was used to play back the pattern of the trace, creating sound.

In 1877, Edison recorded the words "Mary had a little lamb" on his phonograph. When they heard his voice played back on the phonograph, Edison's assistants accused him of tricking them. When Edison demonstrated his machine to the general public, they thought it was magical, leading the press to call him "The Wizard of Menlo Park."

With the invention of the phonograph, Thomas Edison became famous around the world. He toured the country with his new invention and was invited to the White House to demonstrate it to President Rutherford B. Hayes. Though Edison's phonograph was a success, he continued to work on improving it.

Making Movies

Edison was eager to develop a machine that recorded and played back moving pictures, much like the phonograph recorded sound. The result was the kinetograph and the kinetoscope.

The kinetograph could record any action, such as a person sneezing or a cat jumping. It took photographs one after another, at a quick speed of 46 photographs per second. Then the kinetoscope played back the sequence of pictures at a fast speed, creating an illusion of motion, much like a flip book.

The kinetoscope was limited. Basically, it was a small box inside in which the movie was projected, or shown. To watch it, you looked through a little peephole.

Edison knew that to make a profit, he had to develop a projector to show images that an entire audience could view. Such a projector already existed in Europe. So Edison worked with European inventors to develop the vitascope in 1896. Audiences loved it. When a film called *Rough Sea at Dover* was shown, people sitting in the front row actually jumped back during scenes of crashing waves. They were afraid they would get wet!

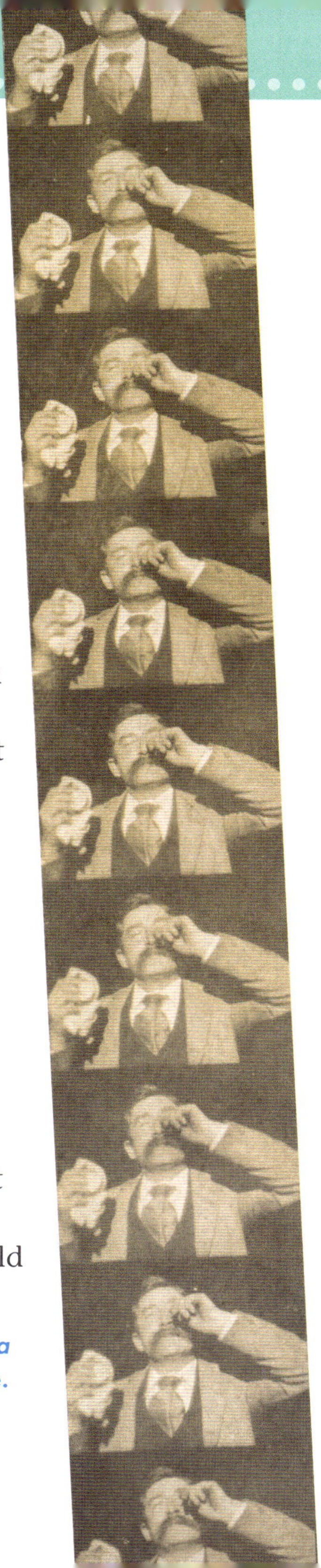

This is one frame from *Record of a Sneeze*, the first film Edison made.

The Electric Light Bulb

If the phonograph was Edison's favorite invention, the electric light bulb is the one people best remember him for. However, Edison was not the first person to experiment with electric light. Electric lights called arc lights already lit up city streets, but they were very bright. Edison invented a practical light bulb, one that eventually replaced gas lights and candles in people's homes.

Edison spent years working on his light bulb. He hired a glassmaker to experiment with differently shaped bulbs until they found a shape that worked. Then Edison searched for a suitable material to use for the **filament**, the tiny wire that glows inside the bulb. He tried 1,600 different materials, including fishing line and human hair! But then, in 1879, he watched as a piece of burnt thread glowed for 40 hours inside a glass bulb. That was the result he had been waiting for. Edison knew then that he had developed the first practical light bulb.

Thomas Edison's first successful light bulb

An Electric System

Edison had a plan to light up the world. The lightbulb was only the first step in the plan. After all, lightbulbs need **sockets**, wiring, switches, and power, so Edison began working on an entire system. It was a huge project, but Edison was not discouraged. He wanted to make electricity available to everyone—at a reasonable price, of course. "We will make electricity so cheap, only the rich will burn candles!" he said.

Edison and his team worked hard on the electric power system. They developed generators to produce the electricity and wires to carry it from power stations to buildings. Because profit was always important to Edison, he developed meters that measured the amount of electricity people used so he could charge them for it.

In 1882, Edison tested his system. At his Pearl Street Station in New York City, Edison flipped a switch, sending electricity to light up 25 buildings.

The age of electric light had begun, but not everyone could throw out their candles. Another 50 years went by before more than half of Americans had electric power in their homes. Still, Edison was the one man who had helped make it all possible.

A view inside Edison's Pearl Street Station

The Laboratory at West Orange

At its peak during World War I (1914–1918), the West Orange laboratory and factory employed 10,000 people.

In 1886, Edison began building a new laboratory in West Orange, New Jersey. He bragged that the laboratory contained everything necessary to invent "useful things every man, woman, and child in the world wants . . . at a price they could afford to pay."

The place was huge, ten times bigger than the laboratory at Menlo Park. The extra space allowed Edison and his team to work on many more projects than they had at Menlo Park. It also allowed them to employ many more people. Eventually, Edison had factories built near the laboratory so that new inventions could be **manufactured** in large quantities and then sold around the world. Edison's invention business was bigger than ever!

The Talking Doll

Not all of Edison's inventions were successful. One example is the talking doll. Edison had the idea to record nursery rhymes on tiny phonographs that fit inside a doll. But the phonographs broke easily, forcing Edison's company to stop making the dolls after just a couple of years.

Thomas Edison (center) with Henry Ford (left), and Harvey Firestone (right)

Final Years

By the time Edison was in his seventies, his health had begun to fail. But even in poor health, he continued to work, going to the laboratory every day.

Edison's last experimental work was done at the request of two of his friends, Henry Ford and Harvey Firestone. Ford was well-known as the man who had developed a successful car manufacturing company. Firestone was one of the first makers of car tires. The men asked Edison to find a new source of rubber to make car tires. Up to that time, natural rubber used for tires came from the rubber tree, which did not grow in the United States. Edison tested thousands of different plants to find a replacement. He was still working on this project at the time of his death on October 18, 1931.

Lasting Achievements

Four days after Edison died, on October 22, 1931, people across the country switched off their electric lights. For 60 seconds they stood in darkness, remembering the man who had made those lights possible. It was a fitting tribute to a great inventor. But it was also a reminder of one of America's great success stories. Born into an ordinary family, Edison turned his ideas into real products through hard work and **persistence**. By the time he was in his thirties, Edison and his inventions were known around the world.

Over his lifetime, Edison received patents for 1,093 inventions. He made it possible to flip a switch and have instant light. His invention of the phonograph paved the way for CD and MP3 players. Movies and television were built on his movie camera and projector. Edison changed the way people live.

In 1928, Congress gave Edison (second from the right, with his wife Mina) a medal to honor his work.

Glossary

filament a thin thread or wire in a light bulb that glows when electricity is sent through it

manufacture to assemble parts into a product in a factory

patent a legal document that prevents others from copying or making money from an invention

persistence not giving up

profit money made by a business after paying its expenses

socket the part of a lamp or light that holds the lightbulb

telegraphy sending and receiving messages by electronic signal over wires

transmitter the part of a telephone that changes sound into electrical signals